INTRAPRENEURSHIP

The Secret Of Entrepreneural Success

Jason Bender

TABLE OF CONTENTS

INTRODUCTION

If you imagine becoming a successful entrepreneur is your achievable dream and focus in the nearest future, you might only partially correct. There are so many challenges faced by entrepreneurs during the very beginning of the business. The only secret of surviving the thorns of entrepreneurship is the mastering of the basic values and skills of intrapreneurship operandi.

According to Richard Branson (The New York business Expert and the founder of the Virgin Group and Companies) in the Business column of National Newspaper tagged "Intrapreneurs: Building for the future" dated on Sunday punch December 5th, 2010, he was being reported as follows;

"Virgin could never have grown from student magazine to the group of more than 200 companies it is now, were it not for a steady stream of intrapreneurs who looked for and developed opportunities, often leading efforts that went against the

grain. One example that springs to mind was at Virgin Atlantic, about 10 years ago. None of the big expensive seat design firms seemed able to solve the design problems posed by our specifications for our Upper Class cabin, but a young designer, Joe ferry, volunteered(insistently) to give the project a go .We set him loose, and the herringbone-configured private sleeper suites that resulted from his "outside box" creativity put us year ahead of the pack and made for millions of every happy horizontal fliers"

In today's dynamic and ever-evolving business landscape, the role of entrepreneurship extends beyond traditional startup ventures. Increasingly, organizations are recognizing the value of fostering an entrepreneural spirit within their own ranks through the concept of intrapreneurship. Intrapreneurship refers to the cultivation of entrepreneural skills and mindset within employees to drive innovation, create new opportunities, and catalyze organizational growth. Developing intrapreneurship skills is crucial for individuals seeking entrepreneural success within established companies, as it equips them with the tools to think like entrepreneurs, take calculated risks, and transform ideas into tangible results.

In this context, understanding the key intrapreneurship skills and their application within organizational settings is paramount to harnessing the full potential of entrepreneural talent and driving sustainable innovation.

In today's rapidly evolving business landscape, the line between entrepreneurship and intrapreneurship is becoming increasingly blurred. While entrepreneurship traditionally refers to starting new ventures, intrapreneurship focuses on fostering innovation and entrepreneural thinking within existing organizations.

Intrapreneurship has emerged as a vital driver of success, enabling companies to adapt, innovate, and thrive in the face of disruptive change.

The skills and mindset associated with intrapreneurship are essential not only for aspiring entrepreneurs but also for professionals within established organizations who seek to create value, drive innovation, and seize new opportunities. Intrapreneurship skills empower individuals to think and act like entrepreneurs, even within the constraints of corporate environments. They enable employees to identify unmet needs, challenge the status quo, and drive forward-thinking initiatives that can lead to transformative outcomes.

The success of intrapreneurship hinges on a diverse set of skills that encompass creativity, risk-taking, adaptability, and strategic thinking. Intrapreneurs are adept at identifying emerging trends, market gaps, and untapped opportunities within their organizations. They possess the ability to envision new possibilities, develop innovative solutions, and effectively communicate their ideas to stakeholders. Moreover, they demonstrate resilience in the face of setbacks and embrace a growth mindset that fuels continuous learning and improvement.

Intrapreneurship skills also encompass the ability to navigate organizational dynamics, influence stakeholders, and foster collaboration.

Intrapreneurs understand the importance of building relationships, networking, and engaging with cross-functional teams to garner support for their initiatives. They leverage their communication and interpersonal skills to inspire and mobilize others toward a shared vision, fostering an entrepreneural culture that encourages creativity and innovation throughout the organization.

Furthermore, intrapreneurship skills are closely tied to the ability to manage and mitigate risk. Intrapreneurs possess a calculated approach to risk-taking, carefully assessing potential challenges and opportunities while balancing the need for innovation with the realities of the business environment. They are comfortable with ambiguity and uncertainty, embracing experimentation and iteration as they navigate uncharted territories within their organizations.

The impact of intrapreneurship extends beyond individual career growth and organizational success. Companies that foster intrapreneurship create environments that attract and retain top talent, as they provide employees with opportunities for growth, empowerment, and autonomy. Intrapreneurship fuels a culture of innovation and agility, enabling organizations to stay ahead of the curve and seize emerging opportunities in a rapidly changing marketplace.

Virtually, intrapreneurship skills have become indispensable for entrepreneural success in today's dynamic business landscape. Whether one aims to launch a startup or drive innovation within an established organization, cultivating intrapreneural skills empowers individuals to ignite change, seize opportunities, and create value. The fusion of entrepreneural thinking and corporate environments holds the key to unlocking untapped potential, driving innovation, and propelling organizations toward sustained success.

CHAPTER ONE

What Is Intrapreneurship?

The concept of intrapreneurship is not new, and it has been around since the 1980s when it was first coined by Gifford Pinchot III. In recent years, however, it has gained more attention as companies strive to remain competitive and adapt to changing market conditions.

Intrapreneurship involves creating an environment where employees are encouraged to take calculated risks and think outside the box. It provides a platform for employees to share their ideas, collaborate with others, and develop their skills. This approach can lead to increased employee engagement, improved productivity, and more innovative solutions.

Intrapreneurs often have a different mindset than traditional employees. They are willing to challenge the status quo and take calculated risks to achieve their goals. They also tend to be more agile and adaptable, which can be a significant advantage in a rapidly changing business environment.

There are several benefits of intrapreneurship for organizations. First, it can lead to the development of new products and services that can help the company remain competitive. Second, it can foster a culture of innovation, which can lead to increased employee engagement and satisfaction. Finally, it can help the organization attract and retain top talent who are attracted to companies that encourage creativity and innovation.

To implement an intrapreneurship program, organizations must create an environment that fosters creativity and innovation. This can involve providing resources such as time, money, and technology to support employee ideas. It can also involve creating cross-functional teams to encourage collaboration and idea sharing.

Intrapreneurship is an approach that can help organizations remain competitive and adapt to changing market conditions. By creating an environment that fosters creativity and innovation, organizations can empower their employees to take risks and develop new ideas that can lead to significant business growth.

Intrapreneurship refers to the practice of promoting entrepreneurship within an organization or company. This involves encouraging employees to take initiatives, be creative, and come up with innovative solutions to problems. Intrapreneurs are individuals within a company who have an entrepreneurial mindset and are willing to take risks to drive growth and innovation.
They work alongside other employees in the company and are often given resources to pursue their ideas and develop new products or services. Intrapreneurship can lead to increased innovation, improved processes, and a more engaged and empowered workforceAlso according to Journal of small business enterprise under the section " Clarifying the intrapreneurship concept" the

author, Robert D. made the following clarifications:

*"**Intrapreneurship is more precisely defined by referring to emergent behavioral intentions and behaviors that are related to departures from the customary ways of doing business in existing organizations**"*

Therefore, for every ramification, intrapreneurship enables organizations to effectively accelerate and manage change. Intrapreneur helps employees to mentally develop while keeping them engaged.

The International Journal of Business Administration write the following under the headings 'Intrapreneurship, Innovation, and Competitiveness in Organization':

*"**To ensure survival, seize opportunities, and resist threats in the unpredictable business scenario, companies increasingly adopt practices that enable**"*

intra-entrepreneur behavior. This behavior is characterized by the alignment of company members in search of innovative solutions for the development of the organization and building a competitive advantage"

- ## Innovation and Creativity

Intrapreneurship is a concept that has been gaining attention in recent years as more and more organizations are recognizing the values of this approach.Intrapreneurship is the process by which an individual, typically an employee of a company, takes an idea and, with the support of the organization, develops it into a business venture.

The concept of intrapreneurship is based on the belief that employees can be creative and innovative and should be given the opportunity to develop and implement their ideas. Intrapreneurs are seen as individuals who have the entrepreneural skills and abilities to develop an idea and create a business, but within the framework of existing organization.Intrapreneurship differs from traditional entrepreneurship in that it takes place within an established organization.

This means that the intrapreneur has access to resources and support from the organization, such as mentorship, capital, and access to customers. Generally, the biggest benefit of intrapreneurship is that it allows organizations to benefit from innovative ideas without the risk of investing in a new venture.Intrapreneurs can equally help organizations to stay ahead of their competition by bringing in new ideas and products.

In order to foster intrapreneurship, organizations need to create an environment that encourages creativity and innovation. This includes providing employees with access to resources and training, as well as creating a culture that rewards and recognizes intrapreneurship.

Organizations should also create systems that allow intrapreneurs to share their ideas and receive feedback from other employees and management.

Intrapreneurship is an important concept for organizations to understand and embrace if they want to stay competitive in today's business world. By creating an environment that encourages creativity and innovation, organizations can benefit from the ideas of their employees and make sure they stay ahead of their competition.

CHAPTER TWO

How To Become A Successful Entrepreneur By Intrapreneurship Skills

As previously stated, the ability of the intrapreneur to take a risk is the most formidable tool of a successful entrepreneur. we may ask ourselves "What are the risks?" A chance of losing something, or something done even if there is fear and chance of danger.

However in business colloqualism, risk may be best described as a network outcome of every work done for the income of goods and services. Because risk is not necessarily a fear or threat for a professional intrapreneur but rather a stepping stone to the next level.

Bear it in mind that risk may be small or big but the most important part is the innovative skills to convert it all to the net growth and development of the organization.

For instance if the first pilot had never risked flying into the air, the inventor of the rocket might still be on the testnet of the launch room or rather an ordinary imagination without motion. Intrapreneurship skills include creative problem solving, effective communication, and ability to take initiative.

Additionally, they involve being able to identify opportunities, being persistent and taking calculated risks.

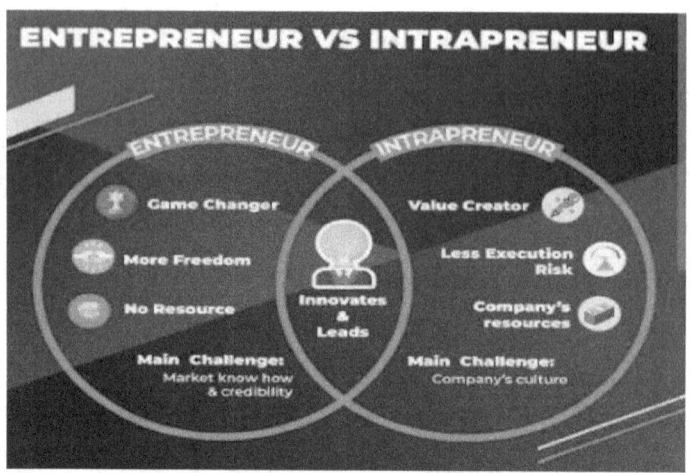

• Planning and Management

In addition, every prospectus and successful intrapreneurs must be a good manager and planner. Management and intrapreneurship could be regarded as the two sides of the same coin. Management is the process of planning, organizing, leading, and controlling resources to achieve organization objectives. Intrapreneurship on the other hand, is the practise of taking on entrepreneurial characteristics and activities within an organization.

Management is an essential part of any organization and is responsible for the efficient and effective use of resources.

It involves setting goals, developing strategies, and making decisions that will help the organization reach its objectives. Intrapreneurship is an important addition to management, as it encourages innovation, risk-taking, and the development of creative solutions. Management and intrapreneurship can work together to create the necessary structure, provide resources, and develop processes and policies that will allow employees to innovate. Meanwhile, intrapreneurship, can be used to foster a culture of creativity, risk-taking, and experimentation. Organizations that embrace both management and intrapreneurship will be better positioned to succeed in a competitive business environment. Management provides the structure and resources needed to achieve success, while intrapreneurship encourages innovation and creativity. By creating an environment where employees are encouraged to take risks and think outside the box, organizations can unlock new sources of value and drive growth.

• Developing Practical Ideas

Intrapreneurs can play a vital role in developing practical ideas for sustainability within their organizations. Here are some steps that intrapreneurs can take to develop practical ideas for sustainability:

Identify sustainability challenges: Intrapreneurs need to start by identifying the sustainability challenges that their organization faces. They can do this by looking at the organization's operations, supply chain, and products and services. They can also conduct a stakeholder analysis to identify the sustainability concerns of customers, employees, and other stakeholders.

Conduct research: Once the challenges are identified, intrapreneurs need to conduct research to understand the root causes and potential solutions. They can review best practices from other organizations, consult with experts, and use data analysis to inform their approach.

Develop a sustainability strategy: Based on the research, intrapreneurs can develop a sustainability strategy that outlines the organization's goals, targets, and actions to address the identified sustainability challenges. The strategy should be aligned with the organization's mission, vision, and values and should have the support of senior management.

Engage stakeholders: Intrapreneurs need to engage stakeholders in the sustainability strategy to ensure buy-in and support. This can involve creating a sustainability team or task force that includes representatives from different departments and levels of the organization. Intrapreneurs can also involve customers, suppliers, and other stakeholders in the strategy development process.

Implement the strategy: Once the strategy is developed, intrapreneurs need to implement it by identifying specific projects, initiatives, and actions. These can include reducing waste, conserving energy and water, improving supply chain sustainability, and developing sustainable products and services.

Measure and monitor progress: Intrapreneurs need to measure and monitor progress to ensure that the sustainability strategy is achieving its goals and targets. This can involve setting up sustainability metrics and reporting mechanisms and regularly reviewing and analyzing data to identify areas for improvement.

By following these steps, intrapreneurs can develop practical ideas for sustainability that can help their organizations become more environmentally and socially responsible while also creating value for stakeholders.

Intrapreneurship is a process of developing practical ideas for products and services within an existing organization. Intrapreneurs are employees who combine the creative spirit of an entrepreneur with the resources of the organization in which they work.

They bring innovative ideas to life and create value for the organization.

Intrapreneurs have the ability to beyond income and come up with creative solutions to existing problems. They also have a strong customer focus and able to understand customer needs and develop solutions that meet those demands.

A key component of entrepreneurship is the ability to develop and execute a plan. Intrapreneurs must able to identify problems, develop solutions, and then implement those solutions respectively.

This requires a combination of creativity, problem solving skills, and project management skills.Intrapreneurs must also be able to work independently and take initiative.

They must be comfortable with taking risks and making decisions without the benefit of guidance from higher-level management. They also need to collaborate with other department and stakeholders in order to develop and implement their ideas.

This requires the ability to track progress and identify areas for improvement.

Intrapreneurs must be able to communicate their progress and successes to higher-level managers and other stakeholders.In summary, Intrapreneurship is essential to the success of any organization and is key to driving innovation and growth to every successful entrepreneur.

CHAPTER THREE

Modeling And Rebranding

From the United States to the extreme border of China, even to the under and developing continents of Africa, Setting up a business is never a a big issue, but the professionalism of driving a business towards intrapreneurship level is the absolute demanding value.

Accordingly, many have succeded in set up of either small or large scale businesses and even earned a very tangible returns of thier overall network input.

However, and on the contrary, little did those people realize that they are only harvesting the unripe fruits of their labor.

Therefore this chapter will guide you towards rebranding by unmasking the hidden treasures, structure and deserving outlook of a successful entrepreneurship model.

IDEALISM - The principle that give absolute modeling to concepts, ideas or innovations. Thus idealism sought to integrate ideas or values into an absolute perfection. considering the types of skills in labor namely, skills, semi skilled and unskilled, the only value that could work for idealism is skilled and no alternatives. hence only and unless the marginal graph of entrepreneur meet the demand point of idealism, modeling and rebranding a successful intrapreneurship could be very far reaching.

Therefore a good intrapreneur always idealistic in nature and find best skilled labour to do the job.

Business modelling and rebranding is an essential part of any successful business. It involves taking an in-depth look at the business and evaluating its current state and potential for growth, then developing an effective model for the fulture and rebranding the business to reflect its new identity.

• Business Modeling

Entrepreneurship and modelling may seem like two different worlds, but in reality, they share many similarities. Both require creativity, innovation, risk-taking, and a strong work ethic to succeed. In this article, we'll explore how entrepreneurship and modelling intersect and how the skills of one can benefit the other.

Entrepreneurship is the process of creating or starting a new business venture. It involves identifying an opportunity, developing a business plan, securing financing, and executing the plan. Successful entrepreneurs must be creative, innovative, and willing to take risks to achieve their goals.

Similarly, modelling is a highly competitive and demanding industry that requires creativity, innovation, and risk-taking. Models must constantly adapt to changing trends, work hard to maintain their appearance and health, and take advantage of opportunities to advance their careers.

One way that entrepreneurship and modelling intersect is in the development of a personal brand. Just as entrepreneurs must create a strong brand identity for their business, models must develop a personal brand that sets them apart from others in the industry. This involves identifying their unique strengths, values, and personality traits and using them to create a cohesive image and message.

Entrepreneurship can also benefit modelling by providing models with the skills and mindset to succeed in a highly competitive industry. For example, entrepreneurs must be highly organized and able to manage multiple tasks simultaneously.

This skill is essential for models who must balance photoshoots, castings, and other engagements while also maintaining their personal lives.

Entrepreneurship also requires strong networking skills, which can benefit models who must build relationships with photographers, agents, and other industry professionals. Models who have an entrepreneural mindset are more likely to proactively seek out new opportunities and develop strong relationships with key stakeholders.

Finally, entrepreneurship can provide models with the skills and knowledge to launch their own businesses or pursue entrepreneural ventures within the modelling industry. For example, a model who has developed a personal brand and has experience in marketing and finance may be well-suited to start their own modelling agency or fashion line.

In view of this, entrepreneurship and modeling share many similarities and can complement each other in meaningful ways. Models who develop an entrepreneural mindset and skills will be better equipped to succeed in a highly competitive industry and may even be able to launch their own ventures. By embracing the principles of entrepreneurship, models can take their careers to the next level and achieve their goals

A business requires an understanding of intrapreneurship models such as; the customer values and the competitive landscape in order to determine the most effective way to move business forward.Also it involves making decisions about products and services offered, the target market, and the pricing structure.

In entrepreneurship, individuals create new businesses or products, taking on the risks and rewards of being their own boss. Similarly, in modelling, individuals create a brand around themselves and their image, taking on the risks and rewards of being in the public eye.

Entrepreneurship and modelling both require individuals to constantly adapt and evolve. In entrepreneurship, this may involve pivoting to a new business model or product line in response to changes in the market. In modelling, this may involve adapting to new trends and styles in the fashion industry.

Both fields also require individuals to have a strong sense of self-confidence and the ability to persevere in the face of challenges. In entrepreneurship, this may involve overcoming funding obstacles or navigating
regulatory hurdles. In modelling, this may involve dealing with rejection or criticism in the pursuit of success.

In both entrepreneurship and modelling, success is often determined by the ability to effectively market oneself or one's business. Entrepreneurs must be able to effectively communicate their value proposition to potential customers, while models must be able to market their image to agencies and clients.

Finally, both fields require a willingness to take risks in pursuit of one's goals. Entrepreneurs must be willing to invest time, money, and resources in their business, while models must be willing to take on new and challenging assignments in order to build their brand and reputation.

Herefore, while entrepreneurship and modelling may seem like disparate fields, they share many common traits and require similar skills and mindsets for success. Both require creativity, innovation, adaptability, confidence, effective marketing, and a willingness to take risks. Whether you are starting a new business or pursuing a career in modelling, embracing these traits can help you achieve your goals and become a successful entrepreneur or model.

• Rebranding

Rebranding is the part of business modeling that deals with changing the structural outlook of the business. The customers usually get bored and becoming un-interested in unpolished business outlook and environs. This can be easily overcome by creating a new logo, website, upgrading reception and marketing offices and other visual elements, as well as developing a tagline and other messaging to help customers understand the buisiness's new identity.

Intrapreneurship and rebranding are two concepts that may seem unrelated, but they are actually closely intertwined.

Thus and as previously pinpointed, intrapreneurship refers to the act of employees within an organization taking on an entrepreneurial mindset, driving innovation and growth within the company. Rebranding, on the other hand, is the process of refreshing or changing a company's brand image and messaging in order to better align with its goals and values. In this article, we will explore how intrapreneurship and rebranding can work together to create a more successful and dynamic enterprise.

First, intrapreneurship can be a catalyst for rebranding. When employees take on an entrepreneural mindset, they may identify areas where the company's brand image and messaging could be improved or refreshed. By encouraging employees to think creatively and take risks, organizations can leverage the insights and ideas of their team members to drive a successful rebranding effort.

Second, rebranding can support intrapreneurship by giving employees a fresh perspective on the company's goals and values. When a company undergoes a rebranding effort, it is an opportunity to clarify its mission, vision, and values.
This can help employees understand the company's direction and goals more clearly, and inspire them to think creatively about how to achieve those goals.

Third, both intrapreneurship and rebranding require a willingness to take risks and embrace change. By fostering a culture of innovation and experimentation, organizations can encourage employees to think outside the box and take risks in pursuit of new ideas and opportunities. Similarly, by embracing a rebranding effort, organizations demonstrate their willingness to adapt and evolve in response to changing market conditions and customer needs.

Finally, both intrapreneurship and rebranding can lead to increased competitiveness and growth for organizations. By empowering employees to think creatively and pursue new ideas, companies can stay ahead of the curve in terms of innovation and customer value. And by refreshing its brand image and messaging, an organization can better connect with its target audience and differentiate itself from competitors.

Therefore, intrapreneurship and rebranding are two powerful tools that can help organizations stay competitive, grow, and thrive. By embracing both concepts, companies can create a culture of innovation, inspire employees to think creatively, clarify their goals and values, and differentiate themselves from competitors. Whether you are a startup or a well-established organization, intrapreneurship and rebranding can help you achieve your goals and stay ahead of the curve in an ever-changing business landscape.

However, business modeling and rebranding can be a challenging process, but it is also rewarding. It takes time and effort to create a successful business model that can help the business grow and thrive. But with the right model rebranding through qualified and competent intrapreneural skills, business can be strategically rebranded into the long-term success.

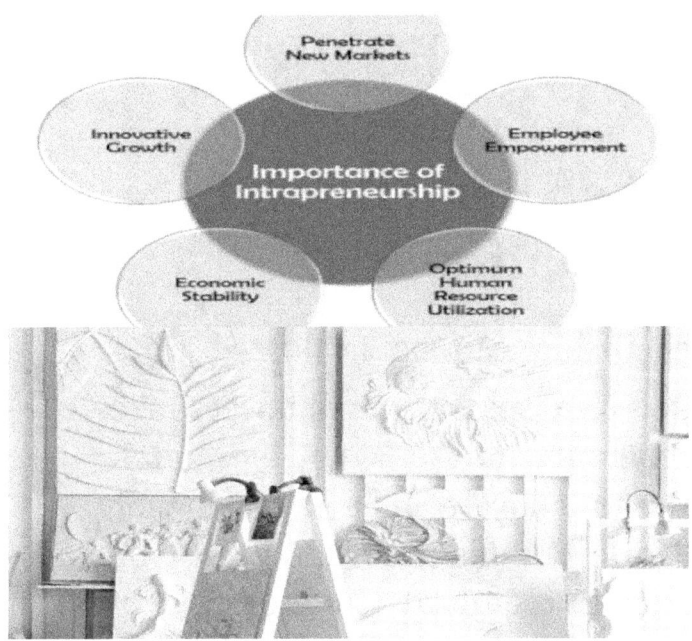

CHAPTER FOUR

Customer Priority and Relations

First, intrapreneurship can be facilitated by a customer-oriented mindset. When employees take on an entrepreneural mindset, they are often driven by a desire to innovate and create value for the company. However, this innovation must be focused on meeting the needs and desires of customers in order to be successful.

A customer-oriented mindset ensures that the needs and desires of customers are at the forefront of intrapreneural initiatives, which can help to ensure that these initiatives are successful and create value for the organization.

Second, a customer-oriented mindset can support intrapreneurship by fostering a culture of empathy and understanding. When employees are focused on meeting the needs and desires of customers, they are more likely to listen to and understand the perspectives of others. This can help to create a supportive environment where intrapreneurship can thrive, and where employees are encouraged to take risks and think creatively in order to meet the needs of customers.

Third, both intrapreneurship and a customer-oriented mindset require a willingness to be flexible and adapt to changing circumstances. By being open to feedback from customers and constantly evaluating and refining intrapreneural initiatives, organizations can stay ahead of the curve in terms of innovation and customer value. This can help to create a competitive advantage for the organization, as it is better able to meet the evolving needs and desires of customers.

Finally, both intrapreneurship and a customer-oriented mindset can lead to increased customer loyalty and growth for organizations. By empowering employees to think creatively and pursue new ideas, companies can create innovative products and services that meet the needs and desires of customers. And by maintaining a customer-oriented mindset, organizations can ensure that these products and services are well-received and valued by customers, leading to increased loyalty and growth for the organization.

Intrapreneurship and a customer-oriented mindset are two critical components of a successful and dynamic organization. By fostering a culture of innovation, empathy, and adaptability, companies can encourage employees to take risks, think creatively, and pursue new opportunities for growth and success. And by maintaining a customer-oriented mindset, organizations can ensure that these initiatives are well-received and valued by customers, leading to increased customer loyalty and growth for the organization. Whether you are a startup or a well-established organization, intrapreneurship and a customer-oriented mindset can help you achieve your goals and stay ahead of the curve in an ever-changing business landscape.

It is often said that no business without customers and every entrepreneur need intrapreneurship skills to give the customer the reason to have no other choices for goods and services that catches his/her attention. Good customer service is the cornerstone of any successful business. Intrapreneurs are no exception.

As an intrapreneur, it is important to maintain excellent customer service in order to ensure customer satisfaction, repeat business, and ultimately, long-term success.

Here are some tips for how intrapreneurs can maintain good customer services:

1. Have a customer-oriented mindset.

Instead of seeing customers as a source of income, have a customer-focused mindset that puts customer satisfaction first. Make sure that your customer service strategy is civil and moderate, and maximally tailored to each customer's want and needs.

- **Create customer service plan**

Making sure that you have a well-developed customer service plan can help ensure that customer service is consistent and that customers are treated well each time they interact with you

Becoming a successful entrepreneur requires a combination of technical knowledge, business acumen, and a customer-focused mindset. As a technical professional, you already have the technical knowledge and expertise necessary to develop innovative products or services. However, to turn your technical expertise into a successful business venture, you need to take a few key steps.

Identify a customer need: The first step to becoming a successful entrepreneur is to identify a customer need that you can address with your technical expertise. This could be a problem that your customers are facing, or a gap in the market that you can fill with your innovative product or service.

Validate your idea: Once you have identified a customer need, it's important to validate your idea before investing time and resources into developing your product or service. You can do this by talking to potential customers, conducting market research, and testing your idea in a small-scale pilot project.

Develop a business plan: Once you have validated your idea, you need to develop a business plan that outlines your strategy for turning your idea into a successful business venture. Your business plan should include details on your target market, marketing strategy, revenue model, and financial projections.

Build a strong team: As a technical professional, you may have the technical expertise necessary to develop your product or service, but you may not have the business acumen or marketing expertise necessary to launch and grow your business. To overcome this, you need to build a strong team of professionals with complementary skills and expertise.

Focus on customer satisfaction: Finally, to be successful as an entrepreneur, you need to have a customer-focused mindset. This means placing the needs and desires of your customers at the center of everything you do, from product development to marketing and sales.

By focusing on customer satisfaction, you can build a loyal customer base and grow your business over time.

As a professional entrepreneur, it is essential to understand the market and the industry you are entering. Researching competitors and understanding their strengths and weaknesses can help you gain valuable insights and create a unique value proposition. Knowing your target customer and how to reach them is also key to success.

Next, it is important to create a business plan. This plan should include a mission statement, a market analysis, a list of services or products offered, financial projections, and strategies for marketing and operations. A business plan will also help to secure any necessary financing.

Another key to success is to create a network and build relationships. Networking with potential customers, suppliers, mentors, and other entrepreneurs can provide valuable resources and insight. It is also important to join professional organizations and take advantage of the educational opportunities they offer.

Finally, it is essential to stay organized and have a system for managing tasks. Utilizing project management and time management tools can help to ensure that tasks and deadlines are met. Keeping track of expenses and sales can also help to ensure that budget and profitability goals are met.

By following these steps and staying focused, technical professionals can plan for successful entrepreneurship.

In conclusion, becoming a successful entrepreneur as a technical professional requires a combination of technical expertise, business acumen, and a customer-focused mindset. By identifying a customer need, validating your idea, developing a strong business plan, building a strong team, and focusing on customer satisfaction, you can turn your technical expertise into a successful and profitable business venture.

- **Listen and respond to customers' feedback.**

Customers' feedback can be invaluable and can help you understand where you you can make improvements or adjustments in order to better serve your customers

The ability to listen and respond to customer feedback is an essential skill for any entrepreneur. By taking the time to carefully listen to customer feedback, entrepreneurs can gain valuable insights into their business and identify areas for improvement. Furthermore, responding to customer feedback in a timely, thoughtful manner can help build loyalty and trust with customers and show that their opinions matter.

In order to develop this skill, entrepreneurs should focus on active listening.

1. Active listening:

Active listening involves paying attention to the customer's words and body language, as well as reflecting and understanding their thoughts and feelings. This helps ensure that entrepreneurs are not only hearing what the customer is saying, but also understanding the sentiment behind it. Additionally, entrepreneurs should also ask follow-up questions to gain further clarity and ensure that their understanding of the customer's feedback is accurate.

Active listening is an essential skill for entrepreneurs as it enables them to better understand their customers, employees, and partners. Here are some solutions that entrepreneurs can use to improve their active listening skills:

Practice Empathy: Entrepreneurs should put themselves in their customer's shoes to understand their needs, pain points, and goals. This will help entrepreneurs develop a deeper understanding of their customers and tailor their products or services accordingly.

Ask Open-Ended Questions: Asking open-ended questions encourages customers to provide more detailed and thoughtful responses. This provides entrepreneurs with more valuable feedback that can be used to improve their business.

Take Notes: Taking notes during customer interactions shows customers that entrepreneurs are actively listening and care about their feedback. It also helps entrepreneurs remember important details and follow up on any action items.

Repeat Back: Repeating back what the customer has said shows that the entrepreneur has understood their feedback and is committed to addressing their concerns.

Stay Present: Entrepreneurs should avoid distractions during customer interactions and focus on the conversation at hand. This shows that they value their customer's time and feedback.

Use Technology: Entrepreneurs can use technology such as CRM systems, chatbots, and social media monitoring tools to listen to customer feedback and respond to it in a timely manner. This also helps entrepreneurs track customer interactions and identify trends in feedback.

By using these solutions, entrepreneurs can improve their active listening skills and better understand their customers, which can lead to increased customer satisfaction, loyalty, and business success.

2. Empathy:
When responding to customer feedback, entrepreneurs should strive to be empathetic and understanding. Acknowledge the customer's feelings and thank them for their feedback. Showing that the customer's opinion is valued and taken seriously can go a long way in building trust and loyalty. Additionally, entrepreneurs should take responsibility for any mistakes and offer solutions. Taking an active role in resolving the

customer's issue can help build a positive relationship.

3.Open-Mindedness: Being open to feedback, even when it's negative, helps entrepreneurs identify opportunities for improvement and growth.

In today's competitive business climate, having an entrepreneural and open-minded attitude is essential for success. Solutions that come from a creative, adaptive, and forward-thinking mindset are often more effective than traditional ones. Entrepreneural and open-minded solutions can help businesses remain agile and capitalize on opportunities. They can also help them to stay ahead of the competition and develop innovative solutions that create unique advantages.

A key component of entrepreneural and open-minded solutions is the ability to think outside of the box. This involves looking at existing challenges in new ways and considering different angles and strategies to address them. It also requires businesses to be open to different perspectives and ideas from a range of people. This helps them to identify and capitalize on opportunities that may have been overlooked before.

Entrepreneural and open-minded solutions also require businesses to adopt a flexible, iterative approach. This means being able to adapt quickly to changing business conditions and customer needs. It also means having the courage to take risks and experiment with new ideas. This approach can lead to breakthrough solutions that give a business a competitive edge.

Lastly, entrepreneurial and open-minded solutions require businesses to remain open-minded and receptive to new ideas. This means being open to feedback and criticism, and being willing to take risks and try out new things. By developing a culture of openness and experimentation, businesses can create innovative solutions and stay ahead of the competition.

4. Communication Skills: The ability to clearly and effectively communicate with customers is crucial for building relationships and trust.

The world of entrepreneurship is filled with a variety of opportunities, and communication is at the forefront of many of them. Whether you are a freelancer or a startup entrepreneur, effective communication is essential to success.

Good communication helps to build trust with clients, partners, and other stakeholders, and can make the difference between success and failure in any venture. To ensure success as an entrepreneur, it is essential to have the right communication solutions in place.

In today's business world, there are many communication solutions for entrepreneurs to take advantage of. From video conferencing software to virtual meetings and teleconferencing, the options are vast. For entrepreneurs, it is important to find the right communication solution to suit their needs.

Video conferencing is a great communication solution for entrepreneurs. It allows them to connect with clients, partners, and other stakeholders from anywhere in the world. It can also help to reduce travel costs, increase productivity, and improve collaboration.

Teleconferencing is also a great communication solution for entrepreneurs. It allows them to conduct meetings with multiple people at once, without having to travel or be in the same physical location. Virtual meetings are also an excellent communication solution. They allow entrepreneurs to meet with clients or partners from anywhere in the world.

Social media is another great communication solution for entrepreneurs. It enables them to engage with their target audience, share news and updates, and build relationships with potential customers.

For entrepreneurs, it is important to have the right communication solution in place. It can help to build trust and credibility, increase productivity, and create a successful business. Finding the right communication solution for your business can be a challenge, but with the right communication solutions in place, entrepreneurs can be successful.

5. Analytical Skills: Analyzing customer feedback helps entrepreneurs identify patterns and trends, which can guide business decisions.

The entrepreneural and analytical skills solutions available today are designed to help business owners and their teams to become more successful. These solutions provide guidance, support, and resources to help entrepreneurs develop their businesses and increase their profits.

One way entrepreneurs can benefit from these solutions is by using them to gain a better understanding of their markets and customers. They can use this knowledge to make better decisions and create more effective strategies. Additionally, they can use these solutions to identify and target potential customers, build relationships with them, and develop better customer service strategies.

Analytical skills solutions are also useful for entrepreneurs. They can use these solutions to analyze data, identify trends, and develop strategies to optimize their business operations. They can also use these solutions to monitor the performance of their business, identify areas of improvement, and develop plans to maximize their profits.

Finally, entrepreneurs can use these solutions to create detailed reports, track performance, and measure their progress. These solutions can help them develop insights into their business, make better decisions, and stay ahead of the competition.

Overall, entrepreneural and analytical skills solutions have become an integral part of the success of many businesses. They provide entrepreneurs with the tools and resources to become more successful and increase their profits.

By utilizing these solutions, entrepreneurs can make better decisions, develop better strategies, and maximize their profits.

When it comes to entrepreneurship, it's important to have a clear vision of what success looks like and the steps needed to get there. This requires a combination of creative problem-solving, strategic planning, and a willingness to take risks. To be successful, you must also be able to stay organized and motivated, while keeping a close eye on the competition.

Analytical skills, on the other hand, are essential for becoming an effective leader. This involves being able to analyze data, understand the big picture, and make informed decisions. Having an understanding of basic financial concepts and being able to interpret financial statements are also important.

Having a strong understanding of both analytical and entrepreneural skills is essential for success. When used together, they can help you create a strategy that will help you reach your goals and stay ahead of the competition. By understanding how the two work together, you can create a strategy that will help you reach your goals and stay ahead of the competition.

6. Problem-Solving: Entrepreneurs need to use customer feedback to solve problems and make improvements to their products or services.

7. Adaptability: Being able to adapt to changes in customer needs and preferences is essential for long-term success.

By developing these skills, entrepreneurs can listen and respond to customer feedback effectively, which can help them build a loyal customer base, increase sales, and grow their business.

These techniques can help entrepreneurs develop the skill of listening and responding to customer feedback. By taking the time to actively listen and respond in an understanding manner, entrepreneurs can ensure that their customers are satisfied and build loyalty and trust.

- **Build relationship with customer**

Establishing relationships with your customers will help you to better understand their needs and provide them with the best goods and services. Intrapreneurs, like entrepreneurs, can build long-lasting customer relationships by following these steps:

Focus on Customer Needs: Intrapreneurs should focus on understanding and meeting the needs of their customers. They should aim to provide value to their customers by solving their problems or providing solutions to their needs.

Build Trust: Intrapreneurs should strive to build trust with their customers by delivering on their promises and being transparent in their communication.

Personalize the Customer Experience: Personalization is key to building strong relationships with customers. Intrapreneurs should strive to understand their customers' preferences and tailor their interactions and products to meet those preferences.

Provide Excellent Customer Service: Intrapreneurs should provide exceptional customer service to ensure that their customers are satisfied with their experience. They should be responsive to customer inquiries, complaints, and feedback.

Create a Community: Building a community around the brand can help intrapreneurs foster long-lasting relationships with their customers. This can be achieved through social media, events, and other engagement initiatives.

Continuous Improvement: Intrapreneurs should continually seek to improve their products and services based on customer feedback. This demonstrates a commitment to providing the best possible experience for customers and fosters loyalty.

By following these steps, intrapreneurs can build long-lasting customer relationships, which can lead to increased customer retention, loyalty, and revenue.

- **Be proactive and preponderance**

Being proactive help intrapreneur to address customer needs and anticipate any potential issues before they arise

Intrapreneurs are employees within an organization who exhibit entrepreneural qualities such as creativity, innovation, and risk-taking.

They can be proactive in developing customer solutions by taking the following steps:

Understand the customer's needs: Intrapreneurs need to have a deep understanding of their customers' needs, preferences, and pain points. They can do this by conducting market research, customer interviews, and surveys.

Stay up-to-date with industry trends: Intrapreneurs need to be aware of the latest trends in their industry and how they can apply them to create innovative solutions for customers.

Encourage a culture of experimentation: Intrapreneurs should be encouraged to experiment with new ideas and solutions, even if they may fail initially. This can lead to new insights and innovative solutions for customers.

Collaborate with cross-functional teams: Intrapreneurs should work closely with cross-functional teams, including product development, marketing, and customer service, to ensure that customer solutions are holistic and effective.

Leverage technology: Intrapreneurs should leverage technology such as data analytics, AI, and machine learning to develop innovative solutions that meet customer needs.

Be agile: Intrapreneurs need to be agile and adaptable in their approach to developing customer solutions. They should be willing to pivot their strategies based on customer feedback and changing market conditions.

Overall, intrapreneurs can be proactive in developing customer solutions by understanding customer needs, staying up-to-date with industry trends, encouraging experimentation, collaborating with cross-functional teams, leveraging technology, and being agile in their approach.

- **Effective communication**

As an entrepreneur, effective communication is crucial to your success. It is important to be able to communicate your ideas, goals, and vision clearly to your team, investors, and customers. Here are some effective communication solutions for entrepreneurs:

Develop a clear communication strategy: Create a plan for how you will communicate with your team, investors, and customers. This should include the frequency of communication, the channels you will use (email, phone, video conferencing, etc.), and the type of information you will communicate.

Use simple and concise language: Avoid using jargon or technical terms that may not be easily understood by everyone. Use simple language that everyone can understand.

Be transparent: Be honest and transparent in your communication. This will build trust and credibility with your team, investors, and customers.

Use visuals: Use charts, diagrams, and other visual aids to help communicate complex ideas or data.

Use feedback to improve communication: Ask for feedback on your communication style and adjust your approach as needed.

Build a culture of open communication: Encourage your team to communicate openly and provide feedback to each other. This will create a culture of transparency and accountability.

Overall, effective communication is critical to the success of any business. As an entrepreneur, it is important to develop a communication strategy and use these solutions to communicate effectively with your team, investors, and customers.

Intrapreneurship and effective communication are two concepts that are crucial for the success of any organization. While an intrapreneur is taking on an entrepreneural mindset, driving innovation and growth within the company.

Effective communication, on the other hand, is the ability to convey information clearly and concisely, in a way that is easily understood by others. In this article, we will explore how intrapreneurship and effective communication can work together to create a more successful and dynamic organization.

First, intrapreneurship can be facilitated by effective communication. When employees take on an entrepreneural mindset, they are often driven by a desire to innovate and create value for the company. Effective communication is essential for ensuring that these ideas and initiatives are clearly communicated and understood by others within the organization. This can help to build support for these initiatives, and ensure that they are given the resources and attention they need to succeed.

Second, effective communication can support intrapreneurship by fostering a culture of collaboration and sharing. When employees are able to communicate effectively with one another, they are more likely to share ideas and work together to drive innovation and growth. This can help to create a supportive environment where intrapreneurship can thrive, and where employees are encouraged to take risks and think creatively.

Third, both intrapreneurship and effective communication require a willingness to listen to others and to be open to feedback. By encouraging employees to listen to one another and to be receptive to feedback, organizations can create a culture of continuous learning and improvement. This can help to ensure that intrapreneural initiatives are grounded in a deep understanding of customer needs and market trends, and are more likely to succeed as a result.

Finally, both intrapreneurship and effective communication can lead to increased competitiveness and growth for organizations. By empowering employees to think creatively and pursue new ideas, companies can stay ahead of the curve in terms of innovation and customer value. And by communicating effectively, organizations can ensure that these ideas and initiatives are well-understood and supported by others within the organization.

In conclusion, intrapreneurship and effective communication are two critical components of a successful and dynamic organization. By fostering a culture of innovation, collaboration, and continuous learning, companies can encourage employees to take risks, think creatively, and pursue new opportunities for growth and success. And by communicating effectively, organizations can ensure that these initiatives are well-understood and supported by others within the organization. Whether you are a startup or a well-established organization, intrapreneurship and effective communication can help you achieve your goals and stay ahead of the curve in an ever-changing business landscape.

Focus and make sure you are communicating with your customers regularly and effectively in order to better understand their needs and provide them with the best service. By following these tips, an intrapreneur can ensure that they are providing excellent customer service relations. Good customer service is essential for the prospectus entrepreneurs and intrapreneurs must be sure to prioritize it at all cost.

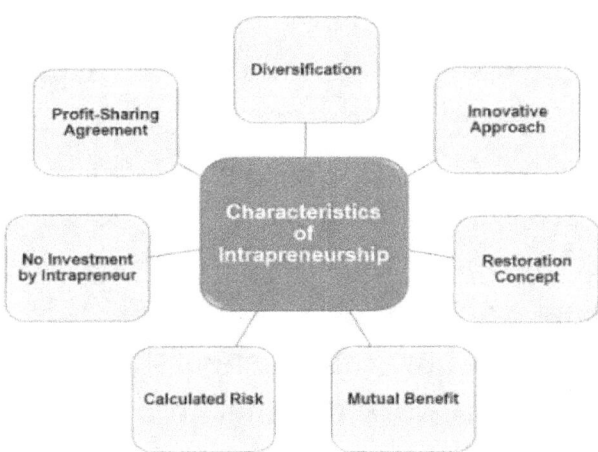

CHAPTER FIVE

The scale of Preference and Decision Making

Intrapreneurship and scales of preference may seem like two unrelated concepts, but they are actually closely connected. Intrapreneurship refers to the act of employees within an organization taking on an entrepreneural mindset, driving innovation and growth within the company.

Scales of preference, on the other hand, refer to the ranking of different options or alternatives based on their perceived value or importance. In this article, we will explore how intrapreneurship and scales of preference can work together to create a more successful and dynamic organization.

First, intrapreneurship can be a valuable tool for identifying and prioritizing the organization's scales of preference. By encouraging employees to think creatively and take risks, companies can leverage the insights and ideas of their team members to identify new opportunities and evaluate different options. This can help organizations rank and prioritize different initiatives based on their potential value or impact. Second, scales of preference can support intrapreneurship by providing a framework for evaluating different ideas and initiatives. By defining the organization's scales of preference, companies can provide employees with a clear understanding of the organization's goals and priorities. This can help employees identify opportunities for innovation and growth that align with the organization's strategic objectives.

Third, both intrapreneurship and scales of preference require a willingness to be flexible and adapt to changing circumstances. By fostering a culture of innovation and experimentation, organizations can encourage employees to think outside the box and take risks in pursuit of new ideas and opportunities. Similarly, by being open to revising and updating its scales of preference, an organization can respond to changes in the market and shifting customer needs.

Finally, both intrapreneurship and scales of preference can lead to increased competitiveness and growth for organizations. By empowering employees to think creatively and pursue new ideas, companies can stay ahead of the curve in terms of innovation and customer value. And by prioritizing its scales of preference, an organization can focus its resources and efforts on the initiatives that are most likely to drive success and growth.

In conclusion, intrapreneurship and scales of preference are two powerful tools that can help organizations stay competitive, grow, and thrive. By embracing both concepts, companies can create a culture of innovation, inspire employees to think creatively, prioritize initiatives based on their potential value, and differentiate themselves from competitors. Whether you are a startup or a well-established organization, intrapreneurship and scales of preference can help you achieve your goals and stay ahead of the curve in an ever-changing business landscape.

The scale of preference is an important concept in decision-making. It allows intrapreneurs and organizations to prioritize different options and outcomes in order to make the best decisions possible. This scale can be used to evaluate any number of criteria, from cost-effectiveness to sustainability to morality. The scale of preference is based on the idea that different preferences are assigned different values.

In other words, some preferences may be given higher priority than others.When used correctly, intrapreneurs use the scale of preference to form decisions that are most likely to achieve their desired outcomes.

• Criteria and Weight

The scale of preference is generally composed of two parts: the **criteria** and the **weight**. The criteria refers to the different aspects of the decision-making process that will be taken into account. For example, a decision about which type of car to purchase might include criteria such as cost, reliability, and fuel-efficiency.The weights refer to the relative importance of each of the given criteria. For example, cost might be given twice as much weight as reliability.

Once the criteria and weights are established, the scale of preference can be used to evaluate different options. However, this is professionally done by an intrapreneur who assigns values to each of the criteria for each option.

For example, a car might be given a value of 5 for cost, 3 for reliability, and 4 for fuel-efficiency.When comparing different options, the option with the highest total value is the one that should be good customer service is the cornerstone of any successful business.

In view of this, the scale of preference is an important tool for decision-making that can help intrapreneurs to prioritize their options in order to make the best decisions possible. By assigning values to different criteria and weighting them accordingly, the preferential scale can provide a helpful framework for understanding the relative importance of different options.

Today many entrepreneurs lack not only the trade mark standard but even the preferential scale of the products and services.The preferential scale as economic determinant of the qualitative and productive values of the company goods and services should never be handled with kid gloves.

• Effective Management for Short and long costs of Production

Effective Management:

Effective management is crucial for the success of any entrepreneur. Here are some ways that entrepreneurs can improve their management skills:

Set clear goals and priorities: Entrepreneurs should have clear goals and priorities for their business. This will help them to focus their efforts and ensure that everyone in the organization is working towards the same objectives.

Build a strong team: Entrepreneurs should build a strong team with complementary skills and expertise. This will ensure that all aspects of the business are covered and that everyone is working towards the same goals.

Communicate effectively: Entrepreneurs should communicate effectively with their team, stakeholders, and customers. This will help to ensure that everyone is on the same page and that issues can be addressed in a timely manner.

Delegate effectively: Entrepreneurs should delegate tasks and responsibilities to their team members effectively. This will help to ensure that everyone is engaged in the work and that the workload is distributed evenly.

Lead by example: Entrepreneurs should lead by example and set the tone for the organization. This will help to establish a positive culture and ensure that everyone is aligned with the values and mission of the business.

Monitor performance: Entrepreneurs should monitor the performance of their team and the business as a whole. This will help to identify areas for improvement and ensure that the business is on track to achieve its goals.

Adapt to change: Entrepreneurs should be adaptable and able to respond to changes in the market, industry, or business environment. This will help to ensure that the business stays relevant and competitive.

Overall, effective management is critical to the success of any entrepreneur. By setting clear goals, building a strong team, communicating effectively, delegating effectively, leading by example, monitoring performance, and adapting to change, entrepreneurs can build sustainable businesses that thrive over the long-term.

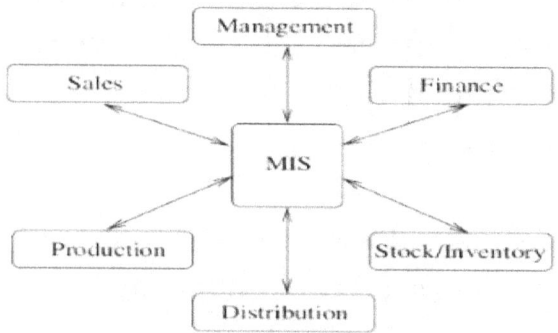

Effective Production:

When intrapreneurship is combined with effective production practices, the results can be powerful.

Effective production is critical for any organization that wants to stay competitive in today's fast-paced business environment. By optimizing production processes, reducing waste, and increasing efficiency, organizations can reduce costs, improve quality, and enhance customer satisfaction. However, achieving these goals requires more than just a focus on efficiency. It requires a culture of innovation, experimentation, and continuous improvement. This is where intrapreneurship comes in.

Intrapreneurs bring a unique perspective to the production process. They are not afraid to challenge the status quo, take risks, and try new things. They are able to identify inefficiencies and bottlenecks in the production process and develop innovative solutions to address them. They are also able to identify new opportunities for growth and expansion.

When intrapreneurs are empowered to apply their skills and expertise to the production process, they can help to drive innovation, improve efficiency, and enhance the overall quality of the products or services being produced. They can also help to create a culture of continuous improvement, where everyone in the organization is encouraged to think creatively and contribute new ideas.

In addition to improving production processes, intrapreneurship can also help organizations to develop new products or services that meet the evolving needs of customers. By leveraging the creativity and innovation of intrapreneurs, organizations can stay ahead of the competition and remain relevant in a rapidly changing market.

Overall, intrapreneurship and effective production go hand in hand. By fostering a culture of intrapreneurship within the organization, organizations can improve production processes, reduce costs, enhance quality, and drive innovation. This can help to create a competitive advantage and position the organization for long-term success in a dynamic and challenging business environment.

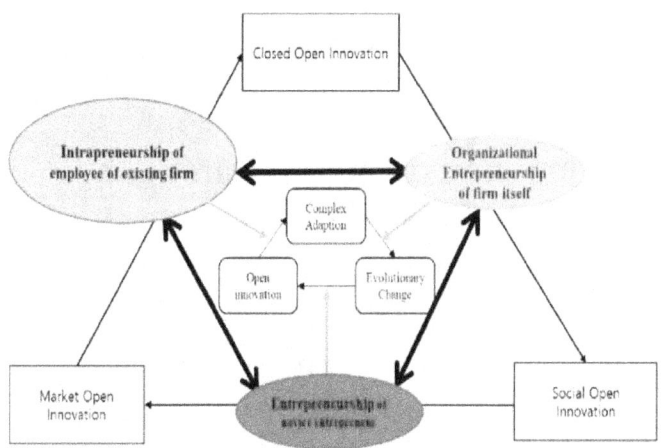

Entrepreneurs can achieve both the short and long costs of production by taking the following steps:

Efficient production processes: Entrepreneurs can implement efficient production processes to reduce the short-term costs of production. By optimizing the production process, they can reduce waste, increase productivity, and reduce labor costs.

Effective cost management: Entrepreneurs can implement effective cost management practices to control short-term costs. This may include negotiating better prices for raw materials, optimizing inventory levels, and managing overhead costs.

Investing in research and development: Entrepreneurs can invest in research and development to create innovative products and processes that reduce the long-term costs of production. By developing new technologies or processes, they can create more efficient production systems and reduce long-term costs.

Training and development of employees: Entrepreneurs can invest in the training and development of their employees to increase their skills and productivity. This can help to reduce labor costs in the short-term and increase the efficiency of the production process in the long-term.

Strategic partnerships: Entrepreneurs can form strategic partnerships with suppliers and other businesses to reduce both short-term and long-term costs. By partnering with suppliers who offer better prices or more efficient delivery systems, they can reduce the short-term costs of production. By forming partnerships with businesses that offer complementary products or services, they can create new opportunities for growth and reduce the long-term costs of production.

Overall, entrepreneurs can achieve both the short and long costs of production by implementing efficient production processes, effective cost management, investing in research and development, training and developing employees, and forming strategic partnerships. By taking a holistic approach to cost management, entrepreneurs can create sustainable businesses that are able to thrive in both the short and long-term.

Long Run and
Short Run
Cost in Business

CONCLUSIONS

In conclusion, "Intrapreneurship: The Secret of Entrepreneural Success" unveils a transformative concept that holds the key to unlocking innovation and driving growth within established organizations. Throughout this book, we have explored the power of intrapreneurship—the entrepreneural mindset and actions exhibited by individuals within corporate settings—and its profound impact on organizational success.

Intrapreneurship empowers employees to think like entrepreneurs, fostering a culture of creativity, risk-taking, and relentless pursuit of groundbreaking ideas. By encouraging intrapreneurship, companies can tap into the immense potential of their workforce, harnessing their talents and aspirations to drive innovation, adapt to change, and stay ahead in today's dynamic business landscape.

We have witnessed how intrapreneurs challenge the status quo, question existing processes, and identify opportunities for disruptive change. Through real-world examples and inspiring case studies, we have seen the extraordinary results that intrapreneurship can achieve—game-changing products, revolutionary strategies, and breakthrough solutions that propel organizations to new heights.

Moreover, intrapreneurship serves as a catalyst for personal growth and professional development. It ignites the entrepreneural spirit within individuals, enabling them to take ownership of their work, unleash their creative potential, and make a meaningful impact. As intrapreneurs, employees become architects of change, driving innovation from within and positioning themselves as invaluable assets to their organizations.

However, implementing and nurturing intrapreneurship is not without its challenges. Organizations must cultivate an environment that fosters and supports intrapreneural initiatives. Leaders must champion a culture that embraces risk-taking, encourages experimentation, and rewards innovative thinking. By doing so, they can create a fertile ground for intrapreneurship to thrive, fostering a dynamic ecosystem of ideas and collaboration.

"Intrapreneurship: The Secret of Entrepreneurial Success" equips both aspiring entrepreneurs and corporate leaders with the tools, strategies, and insights needed to embark on an intrapreneural journey. It highlights the importance of mindset, skillset, and organizational culture in unleashing the true potential of intrapreneurship. Through practical advice, actionable steps, and thought-provoking exercises, this book empowers readers to unlock their intrapreneural spirit and drive meaningful change within their organizations.

As we reach the end of this transformative journey, it becomes clear that intrapreneurship is not merely a buzzword or passing trend—it is the secret ingredient that separates thriving organizations from the stagnant ones. By embracing intrapreneurship, companies can foster a culture of innovation, adaptability, and continuous growth, securing their place at the forefront of their industries.

Now, armed with the knowledge and inspiration found within these pages, it is your turn to become an intrapreneural force, to challenge conventions, and to unleash the entrepreneurial spirit that resides within you. Embrace the power of intrapreneurship, and let it propel you, your organization, and the world towards a future brimming with unlimited possibilities.

As we conclude this journey into the realm of intrapreneurship, it becomes evident that it holds the key to unlocking the secret of entrepreneural success within established organizations. Intrapreneurship is not just a buzzword or a passing trend; it is a powerful force that has the potential to transform stagnant corporations into innovative powerhouses.

Throughout this book, we have explored the fundamental principles of intrapreneurship, examining how it empowers employees to think and act like entrepreneurs within the safety net of an existing organization. We have witnessed the remarkable stories of intrapreneurs who defied the status quo, challenged conventional thinking, and brought about groundbreaking innovations that propelled their companies to new heights.

Intrapreneurship is more than a set of strategies and tools; it is a mindset, a culture that fosters creativity, collaboration, and risk-taking. It encourages individuals to identify opportunities, embrace change, and take ownership of their ideas. By creating an environment that nurtures and rewards intrapreneural behavior, organizations can cultivate a dynamic and adaptable workforce capable of navigating the ever-evolving business landscape.

The benefits of intrapreneurship extend far beyond the immediate success of a single project or initiative. It sparks a ripple effect, inspiring others to embrace their own entrepreneural spirit and contribute to the growth and prosperity of the entire organization. Intrapreneurship creates a virtuous cycle of innovation, where each success fuels the motivation to explore new frontiers, disrupt markets, and redefine industry norms.

However, embracing intrapreneurship does not come without its challenges. Organizations must be willing to break free from the shackles of bureaucracy, hierarchy, and resistance to change. They must provide the necessary resources, autonomy, and support systems to empower their intrapreneurs to thrive. Leaders play a pivotal role in fostering a culture of intrapreneurship by setting a visionary tone, cultivating a sense of purpose, and championing the ideas and initiatives of their intrapreneurs.

The potential for intrapreneurship to shape the future of business is immense. It has the power to revolutionize industries, solve complex societal problems, and drive sustainable growth. By harnessing the collective genius of their employees, organizations can create a competitive advantage that transcends market fluctuations and technological disruptions.

However, we should remember that intrapreneurship is not limited to a select few; it is a mindset that can be cultivated and nurtured within anyone willing to challenge the status quo. It is a call to action for organizations to foster an environment that encourages creativity, collaboration, and calculated risk-taking.

Let this book be the catalyst that sparks your journey towards embracing intrapreneurship. Dare to dream big, empower your employees, and forge a new path towards entrepreneural success from within. The future belongs to those who are willing to break free from the confines of tradition and embrace the spirit of intrapreneurship. Together, we can build a world where innovation knows no bounds, and entrepreneural success becomes a shared reality.

"While it is true that every company needs an entrepreneur to get it , healthy growth requires a smattering of intrapreneurs who drive new projects and explore new and unexpected directions for business development"

RICHARD BRANSON
(CEO AND FOUNDER OF VIRGIN GROUP AND COMPANY)

REFERENCES

1. Richard Branson, CEO of Virgin Atlantic companies

2. Journal of small business enterprise under the section " Clarifying the intrapreneurship concept" the author, Robert D.

3. Gifford Pinchot III. 1980s

4. "Intraprenuer: Building for the future" Nigerial Newspaper, Sunday punch December 5th, 2010,

5. Diagrams and images are from Google search engines